This book is to be returned on or before
the last date stamped below.

1 - FEB 2010

1 1 SEP 2017

Indira GANDHI

ANITA GANERI

Heinemann
LIBRARY

www.heinemann.co.uk/library
Visit our website to find out more information about **Heinemann Library** books.

To order:
☎ Phone 44 (0) 1865 888066
▤ Send a fax to 44 (0) 1865 314091
▭ Visit the Heinemann Bookshop at www.heinemann.co.uk/library to browse our catalogue and order online.

First published in Great Britain by Heinemann Library, Halley Court, Jordan Hill, Oxford OX2 8EJ, part of Harcourt Education.

Heinemann is a registered trademark of Harcourt Education Ltd.

Produced for Heinemann by Discovery Books Ltd
Design: Ian Winton
Editors: Patience Coster, Nicole Irving, Andrew Solway and Jennifer Tubbs
Illustrations: Stefan Chabluk
Picture research: Rachel Tisdale
Production: Séverine Ribierre

Originated by Dot Gradations
Printed and bound in China by South China Printing Company

ISBN 0 431 13881 8
07 06 05 04 03
10 9 8 7 6 5 4 3 2 1

British Library Cataloguing in Publication Data
Ganeri, Anita
  Indira Gandhi. – (Leading lives)
  954'.035'092

A full catalogue record for this book is available from the British Library.

Acknowledgements
The publishers would like to thank the following for permission to reproduce photographs: Bettmann/Corbis: pp. **14, 24, 28, 40, 41, 45, 46, 50, 55**; Corbis: p. **48**; Getty Images: pp. **6, 9, 11, 17, 20, 25, 29, 32, 35, 36**; Hulton-Deutsch Collection/Corbis: pp. **22, 38**; Popperfoto: pp. **4, 37, 43, 52, 54**; Topham/Associated Press: pp. **31, 49, 51**; Topham Picturepoint: pp. **34, 53**.

Cover photograph of Indira Gandhi reproduced with permission of Corbis.

Every effort has been made to contact copyright holders of any material reproduced in this book. Any omissions will be rectified in subsequent printings if notice is given to the publishers.

Contents

Any words appearing in the text in bold, **like this**, are explained in the Glossary.

A new leader for India

The date is 19 January 1966. The place is Delhi, the capital of India, on a cold and misty day. In the central hall of the Indian Parliament, the **Congress Party** of India is gathered to elect a new leader, and to witness history being made. There is an air of intense excitement, for this leader will not only become leader of Congress, but also prime minister of India, and head of the world's largest **democracy**.

As the votes are cast, a tall, slender woman, with dark, brooding eyes, watches proceedings intently. She is Indira Gandhi, the favoured candidate. Indira is dressed simply in a white **khadi sari** and a plain shawl, with a string of brown beads around her neck. The beads are her lucky charm, given to her long ago by a Hindu holy woman. At the entrance to Parliament, someone has presented her with a bouquet of roses, one of which is pinned to her clothes. At last, the votes are counted and the results of the **ballot** announced. Indira has beaten her closest rival by 355 votes to 169. In five days' time, she will officially be sworn in as the first woman prime minister of India.

▲ *Indira Gandhi being sworn in as the first woman prime minister of India.*

TO LOCATE THE PLACES MENTIONED, SEE THE MAP OF INDIA ON PAGE 30.

As the daughter of Jawaharlal Nehru, India's first prime minister, Indira has lived her whole life in the political spotlight, first as Indians struggled to win independence for their country after years of British rule, and later as her father's constant companion. She has seen most of her family jailed as they helped to fight for independence. Indeed, she has spent time in prison herself. But how will she cope with the enormous task that now lies ahead of her? After all, it is extremely rare for an Indian woman to become a politician in such a **male-dominated society**. How will she tackle the problems of poverty and **corruption** that overwhelm the country? What about the fighting between the different religious groups of India that threatens to tear the country apart?

FOR DETAILS ON KEY PEOPLE OF INDIRA GANDHI'S TIME, SEE PAGE 58.

First words as prime minister

'My heart is full and I do not know how to thank you. As I stand before you my thoughts go back to the great leaders: Mahatma Gandhi [the independence leader], at whose feet I grew up, Panditji [Jawaharlal Nehru], my father, and Lal Bahadur Shastri [the second prime minister of India]. These leaders have shown the way, and I want to go along the same path.'

(Indira Gandhi, on becoming prime minister of India, 1966)

All this is for the future. For now, nothing can spoil her moment of triumph. As she leaves Parliament, she is greeted by a cheering crowd. 'Indira Gandhi Zindabad!' they shout. 'Long Live Indira Gandhi!' Indira Gandhi is about to become one of the most powerful women in the world.

2 Birth and family

TO LOCATE THE PLACES MENTIONED, SEE THE MAP OF INDIA ON PAGE 30.

Indira Priyadarshini Nehru was born on 19 November 1917, in the bustling city of Allahabad in northern India. She was the only child of Jawaharlal Nehru, later prime minister of India, and his wife, Kamala. Some of the Nehru women could

▼ *Indira's father, Jawaharlal, as a boy, with his parents, Swaruprani and Motilal Nehru.*

not hide their disappointment that Indira was not a boy. In traditional Indian society, boys were all-important for looking after their parents and carrying on the family line. But Indira's grandfather, Motilal, was irritated by their remarks. 'This daughter of Jawhar, for all you know,' he said, angrily, 'may prove better than a thousand sons.'

The Nehrus

The remarkable Nehru family into which Indira, or Indu as she was known, was born, was a well-off, upper-class **Hindu** family whose **ancestors** came from Kashmir. The head of the family, Motilal Nehru, was one of Allahabad's most brilliant and respected lawyers. Like the rest of the household, Indu was greatly in awe of her grandfather, who could be impatient and quick-tempered; but she also adored him, and he, in turn, spoiled her. She later wrote: 'I was tremendously impressed by my grandfather's bigness. I don't mean physically – but you know, he seemed to embrace the whole world. I loved the way he laughed.'

Indira's grandfather firmly believed in the advantages of a good education, for girls and boys alike. This was unusual because in India at that time it was usually only boys who received an education. Girls stayed at home and helped their mothers with running the household. Motilal had his daughters educated at home by governesses and sent his only son, Jawaharlal, to school and university in England. On his return to India, Jawarharlal joined his father's law practice. Later, both Motilal and Jawaharlal became leading lights in the struggle for India's independence which finally saw an end to British rule. From early childhood, Indira was greatly influenced by her father and grandfather's strong and outspoken political views.

The other members of the Nehru household included Indira's grandmother, Swaruprani; Swaruprani's widowed sister, Bibi Amma; Indira's two aunts, Vijayalakshmi and Krishna; and her mother, Kamala. In addition, there were the servants who looked after the family, and various other friends and relatives who were always coming to stay. In total, the household numbered nearly 100 people.

House of happiness

Indira was born in Motilal's magnificent mansion, Anand Bhavan. This means 'House of happiness' in the **Hindi** language. The huge, rambling house had 42 rooms, surrounded by balconies, and was topped with a decorative dome. From the viewing platform beneath the dome, visitors could admire the imposing grounds with their neatly trimmed lawns, rose garden, orchard, croquet lawn and tennis court. There was even an indoor swimming pool – the height of luxury. Motilal's success as a lawyer meant that he was a wealthy man and no expense was spared. Anand Bhavan was filled with the very best that money could buy – the finest carpets, the best crystal and china, a grand piano, even pedigree dogs. Many items were imported from London. Anand Bhavan was also the first

Kamala Nehru

'Many people know the part which was played by my grandfather and my father [in the independence movement]. But in my opinion, a more important part was played by my mother. When my father wanted to join [Mahatma Gandhi] and... to change our luxurious living, to give up his legal practice, the whole family was against it. It was only my mother's courageous and persistent support and encouragement which enabled him to take the big step which made such a big difference not only to our family but to the history of modern India.'

(Indira Gandhi, writing about her mother's part the Indian independence movement)

▲ *Indira's parents, Jawaharlal and Kamala Nehru, on their wedding day in 1916.*

property in Allahabad to have electricity and running water. Indira later commented that the house was a delightful place for a child to grow up in, with plenty of space to hide and play.

The household at Anand Bhavan was a mixture of East and West. Motilal insisted on wearing Western clothes and speaking English. His wife, Swaruprani, however, was a devout

Hindu who wore a traditional **sari** and spoke Hindi. Anand Bhavan's three kitchens reflected the household's different tastes. They cooked three different types of food – European, Indian vegetarian and Indian non-vegetarian.

A lonely childhood

Despite her family's luxurious lifestyle and the number of people in the household, Indu's childhood was often lonely. Her father and grandfather were hardly ever at home, and there were no other children in the household. Her loneliness was shared by her mother, and the two spent a great deal of time together.

The British Raj

The British Raj is the name given to the time when India was governed by the British. The word 'raj' means 'rule' in Hindi. The Raj officially lasted from 1858 to 1947, although a British company, called the East India Company, controlled large parts of India before this. At the time of Indu's birth, India was part of the British Empire and was governed by the British Parliament and Crown. In London, a secretary of state for India dealt with Indian affairs in Parliament. In India, an official called a **viceroy** acted as the representative of the British king or queen. In the heyday of the British Raj, thousands of British people came to India to live and work. Most Britons kept themselves apart from the Indians, who they considered to be inferior. From the late 19th century, a growing group of Indians began to demand freedom from British rule. In 1885, they formed a political party, called the Indian National Congress, to campaign for independence. Among Congress' leading members were Indira's grandfather, Motilal, and her father, Jawaharlal Nehru.

▲ *King George V of England riding on an elephant during a tiger hunt in India in 1911–12. The British controlled India from 1858 to 1947. Many members of the British Raj led rich and pampered lives.*

Gentle, long-suffering Kamala came from a traditional Hindu family and was not accustomed to European ways. She did not get on well with the other female members of the Nehru family, who looked down on her. They thought she was unsophisticated and not good enough for Jawaharlal. From a very young age, Indu tried to protect and take care of her mother who was frail and often ill. 'We were very close to each other,' Indira later remembered. 'I loved her deeply and when I thought that she was being wronged I fought for her and quarrelled with other people.' Despite her shyness and poor health, Kamala was later to play an important part in India's independence movement.

An uncertain childhood

TO LOCATE THE PLACES MENTIONED, SEE THE MAP OF INDIA ON PAGE 30.

In 1919, when Indu was just two years old, an incident occurred which changed the course of the independence struggle in India, and of Indu's childhood. On 13 April, thousands of Indians gathered in a walled garden in Amritsar to protest peacefully against British rule. A British officer, General Dyer, ordered the crowd to **disperse**. But his troops were blocking the only exit from the garden – there was no way for people to get out. Dyer told his troops to wait for three minutes, then to open fire. In the **massacre** that followed, some 400 people – men, women and children – were brutally killed, and more than a thousand badly injured. At a later enquiry into the massacre, Dyer claimed that he had not known the exit was blocked, but he was removed from his post and sent back to England.

The struggle for freedom

The Amritsar massacre was a turning point for the independence movement, and for the Nehru family. Appalled by the bloodshed, Indians began to realize that they would have to fight for their rights. Both Motilal and Jawaharlal pledged their full support. From now on, Anand Bhavan became a centre of the independence movement. Indu got used to seeing political leaders come and go, at all times of the day and night, eager to talk to her grandfather and father about the struggle for India's freedom.

Mahatma Gandhi

Among the frequent visitors to Anand Bhavan was Mahatma Gandhi, a quiet, modest lawyer, who became the greatest leader of the struggle to get rid of the British and make India a free country again. Gandhi urged Indians not to fight the British with force, but with peaceful protest, or 'satyagraha', which means 'truth force'. First Jawaharlal, and later Motilal, fell under Gandhi's spell. Gandhi became a lasting inspiration throughout Indu's life. No matter how busy he was, he always had time for her. She later wrote: 'He forms part of my earliest memories, and as a very small child, I regarded him not as a great leader but more as an elder of the family to whom I went with difficulties and problems which he treated with grave seriousness which was due to the large-eyed and solemn child I was.' Her aunt also summed up Gandhi's effect on their lives. 'He came, he saw and he conquered. My brother has called [Gandhi's] entry into politics a gentle breeze. That makes me laugh because he came into our family like a hurricane.'

Boycott bonfires

In the aftermath of the Amritsar massacre, Gandhi stepped up his campaign. He called on Indians to **boycott** British goods, refuse to pay their taxes and stop using British-run schools, colleges and law courts. In common with many other Indians who left well-paid jobs which required them to work with the British, Motilal and Jawharlal gave up their legal practice to concentrate on politics. At Anand Bhavan, the boycott began in earnest. One of Indu's earliest memories was of a huge bonfire upon which the family's British-made clothes and other possessions, including her own favourite doll, were ceremonially burned.

From now on, instead of Western clothes, the Nehru family wore Indian clothes made from coarse, white **khadi** cloth. Young Indu was usually dressed in a boy's khadi uniform (trousers, tunic, waistcoat and **Gandhi cap**) of a Congress volunteer. She was often mistaken for a boy.

▲ *Followers of Gandhi burning a pile of British-made cloth in the 1920s.*

'Everybody has gone to jail'

These were unsettling times for Indu. Her grandfather, father, aunts, and later, her mother, were frequently arrested and sent to prison for their part in the freedom movement. A story goes that, one day, visitors arrived at Anand Bhavan. Indu opened the door to them and announced: 'Everyone has gone to jail.' In 1921, when Indu was just four years old, she attended her first trial. She sat on Motilal's knee in the **dock** in the courtroom and listened intently as Motilal and Jawaharlal were both sentenced to six months in jail.

For many years, Indu saw her father very little because he spent so much time in prison. The only contact she had with Jawaharlal was in the form of hundreds of letters which he wrote to her from jail, and which she treasured. The letters were later published in a book, *Glimpses From World History*. They were meant to be educational for Indu, charting the whole of human history. But Jawaharlal also wrote them because he felt guilty at spending so much time away from his daughter.

Playing politics

Even though Indu was often alone, she was proud of what her family were doing. She even tried to join in. While other children of her age were playing games, Indu was playing at politics. She would arrange her dolls into groups of **freedom fighters** and police, and act out protests. She would round up the servants at Anand Bhavan and give rousing speeches about satyagraha. One day, her aunt found

An insecure childhood

'As a child, when the freedom struggle was on, the house was being constantly raided by police, our goods and chattels [possessions] being confiscated, we were being arrested... and I was all part of it.... It was an extremely insecure childhood. One did not know from day to day who would be alive, who would be in the house and what would happen next.'

(Indira Gandhi in 1971, reflecting on her childhood)

her standing on the **verandah**, pretending to be Joan of Arc, the French saint and heroine. Indu said that she had been reading about her and wanted to lead the Indian people to freedom, just as Joan of Arc had done in France.

Motilal and Jawaharlal refused to pay the fines demanded by the courts. So the police were sent to Anand Bhavan to seize valuables instead. Even though she was very young, Indu was furious. She shouted at the policemen to leave things alone, and once nearly cut off an officer's thumb with a bread slicer.

Be brave

'You remember how fascinated you were when you first read the story of Jeanne d'Arc [Joan of Arc] and how your ambition was to do something like her? One little test I shall ask you to apply whenever you are in doubt. Never do anything in secret or anything you wish to hide. For, the desire that you want to hide anything means that you are afraid, and fear is a bad thing and unworthy of you. Be brave, and all the rest follows.'

(Jawaharlal Nehru, in a letter written to Indira from jail)

4 Growing up

When Indira was seven years old, her grandfather sent her to St Cecilia's School in Allahabad. But she did not stay there long. Her father was furious about the choice of school, which was run by three British women. Jawaharlal argued that this contradicted the family's British **boycott**. So Indu was taken away from school and taught at home by Indian tutors.

▼ Indira (left), aged about 12, sitting next to her father, Jawaharlal Nehru.

This pattern continued throughout her schooldays. Her father's jail terms and her mother's poor health meant that she never attended one school for long. But she didn't really mind. She felt out of place at St Cecilia's because she was shy and skinny, and the only girl who wore **khadi** clothes. Besides, she learned more at home than at school – by sitting in the trees in the Anand Bhavan garden, reading books from her grandfather's library, and by listening in on conversations.

Towards the end of 1925, Indu's mother, Kamala, became very ill with **tuberculosis**. Her doctors advised her to go abroad to Switzerland for treatment. In March 1926, Indu and her parents sailed from Bombay for Europe. She was away for almost two years. In Switzerland, Indu attended the International School in Geneva. The school was housed in a Swiss chalet, with stunning mountain views. There, Indu learned French, music and skiing. Later, when Kamala was moved to a **sanatorium** high up in the Alps, Indu was enrolled at a school in Bex, a town closer to her parents. This was a magical time for Indu. She travelled with her parents to Venice, Paris, London and Berlin, and was amazed at the wealth of the cities of Europe, compared with India. But best of all she had both her parents with her – for one of the very few times in her life.

To locate the places mentioned, see the map of India on page 30.

Monkey Army

By the end of 1927, Kamala was well enough to return to India. In 1929, Jawaharlal succeeded Motilal as Congress president. Indu accompanied her father to the Congress meeting in Lahore where he was officially proclaimed president. Back home, she proudly watched him draft a document that set out Congress's promise to work for full independence from Britain. When Jawaharlal had finished, he gave Indu the document to read aloud.

Indu desperately wanted to take part in the independence movement. But at twelve years of age, she was too young to join Congress. Instead, she formed her own organization for children, called the Monkey Army. It was named after the army of monkeys in the **Hindu** sacred text, the *Ramayana*, who helped the god, Rama, to rescue his wife from a demon-king. Several thousand children joined. They ran errands for the adult Congress volunteers, handed out leaflets, put up posters, and carried secret messages. The police were too busy arresting the adults to take any notice of a bunch of children!

Travels and tragedy

In February 1931, tragedy struck. After a short illness, Indira's grandfather, Motilal Nehru, died. Indira was heartbroken. Her grandfather had been one of the most important people in her life and she missed him terribly. Afterwards, Indu was sent away to school in Poona but she was not happy there. With her grandfather gone, her father in prison and her mother often ill, Indu felt more homesick and lonely than ever.

Monkey business

'In their own way, the children also acted as an intelligence group [spies], because frequently the policemen sitting in front of the police station would talk about what was going on, who was to be arrested, where there would be a raid and so on. And four or five children playing hopscotch outside would attract no one's attention. And they would deliver this news to the people in the movement.'

(Indira, talking about the Monkey Army)

▲ *The great Indian poet, philosopher and writer, Rabindranath Tagore. He founded the university at Santiniketan, where Indira studied.*

To locate the places mentioned, see the map of India on page 30.

Indu left school in 1934 and enrolled as a student at Santiniketan, the 'Abode of Peace', the school and university founded by the great Indian poet and philosopher, Rabindranath Tagore in Bengal. She loved the peace and quiet of Santiniketan and was in awe of Tagore. She quickly adapted to the tough living conditions, sleeping on a mat on the floor and taking cold baths. Classes began at 7 a.m. Indu's favourite class was Indian dance and she became an accomplished performer in just a few months. But her happiness did not last long. As Indu was rehearsing for a dance performance, a telegram arrived. Her mother's health had broken down again and she had to leave for Europe as soon as possible. With a heavy heart, Indu packed her bags and said her goodbyes.

Indu and Kamala arrived in Europe in June 1935, then travelled to a sanatorium in southern Germany. It was a depressing place for Indu and she became worn out by the strain of looking after her mother. But Kamala's health continued to deteriorate and she asked to be moved to Lausanne, Switzerland. She died there on 28 February 1936, aged just 36. Jawaharlal, who had been released from prison to be with his wife, was with Indu at Kamala's bedside. Indu was devastated by her mother's death. She felt more alone than ever. For years, she and Kamala had looked after each other. Who could she turn to now?

Rare qualities

'Kamala possessed qualities rarely found in other women. I am hoping that all these qualities of Kamala will be manifest in you in equal measure. May God give you long life and strength to emulate her virtues.'

(Mahatma Gandhi in a letter to Indira on the death of her mother)

England

After Kamala's death, it was decided that Indu should go to school and university in England. In October 1936, she started at Badminton School in Bristol to prepare for the Oxford University entrance exam. The headmistress of the school was a great admirer of Indira's father. A fellow pupil remembers that Indu looked very frail and unhappy, and couldn't wait to go back home to India. Indu herself complained to her father that she found the school rules stifling.

A year later, Indu went to Somerville College, Oxford, to study history. She settled in well, although she did not like the academic work. In Oxford and London, she got to know many Indian students who were eager to meet Nehru's daughter. Among them was Feroze Gandhi (no relation of Mahatma Gandhi). Feroze was a family friend who was active in Congress and had been devoted to Kamala. In England, his friendship with Indu quickly blossomed into love.

▼ *Indira and her father in 1937, leaving Bombay for England where Indira would study at Somerville College, Oxford.*

Marriage

In 1941, as World War Two engulfed Europe, Indira and Feroze decided to leave London and return to India. They caught the slow boat to Bombay via the Cape of Good Hope. On the way, they stopped in Durban, South Africa, where Indira was warmly welcomed by the city's large Indian community. They asked Indira to speak at a reception in her honour. Reluctantly, she agreed – she was not used to speaking in public. But driving around Durban she was appalled to see the desperate conditions in which black people lived under the country's racist regime.

That evening, Indira was so angry she forgot to be tongue-tied. She lectured her Indian audience on the evils of the regime, and criticized them for not doing more to help black people fight against it. Her speech did not go down well!

Marriage

Back home, Indira told her father that she intended to marry Feroze as soon as possible. Nehru was not pleased. He told Indira not to rush into anything. In fact he did not think Feroze was good enough for her. For one thing, Feroze came from a poor family. He did not share Indira's wealthy background. But when it became clear that Indira had made up her mind, Nehru asked her to consult Mahatma Gandhi. If Gandhi agreed to the match, Nehru would not object. After seeing both Indira and Feroze, Gandhi gave his blessing. Not everyone was in favour, though. News of Indira's engagement filled the newspapers and many people were hostile. They were outraged that Nehru was allowing his daughter, a **Hindu**, to marry Feroze, a **Parsi**. In India, at that time, most people married someone who belonged to the same religion as they did.

▲ *Indira (right) and Feroze Gandhi (left) on their wedding day on 26 March 1942.*

Indira and Feroze were married on 26 March 1942 in the grounds of Anand Bhavan. Indira was dressed simply in a **khadi sari** woven by her father during one of his stays in prison. Feroze wore the khadi dress of Congress. The ceremony was traditionally Hindu. Indira and Feroze took seven steps around the sacred fire, and vowed to love and care for each other for the rest of their lives. But Indira also made another vow – to fight against those who tried to take her country's freedom away.

TO LOCATE THE PLACES MENTIONED, SEE THE MAP OF INDIA ON PAGE 30.

Quit India

After their wedding, Indira and Feroze left for a two-month honeymoon in Kashmir. It was a magical time for them both. 'Truly if there is a heaven,' Indira wrote, 'it must be this...' But no sooner were they back than they were thrown into political life once more.

Millions of Indians were fighting for Britain in World War Two, in return for the promise of independence for India. So far, these promises had not been kept. In August 1942, Mahatma Gandhi launched the 'Quit India' movement. If the British did not leave India at once, there would be another campaign of mass civil disobedience. In an effort to control the situation, the British immediately arrested the Congress leaders, including Gandhi and Nehru. Thousands of protestors were imprisoned without trial. But it did not stop the strikes, protests and rioting which swept through India.

▼ *Indira's father, Jawaharlal Nehru, with Mahatma Gandhi in 1946.*

Prison

Indira and Feroze were both active members of the **Congress Party**. They threw themselves into the 'Quit India' campaign. In September 1942, Indira spoke at a public meeting, even though the British government had banned such gatherings. She and Feroze were arrested. Indira was taken to Naini Jail in Allahabad where her father had often been held. Indira did not find prison life easy. 'The ground, the walls, everything around us is mud-coloured,' Indira wrote, 'and so became our jailwashed clothes.' But she was glad to be there. Almost everyone she knew had been to prison. She kept her spirits up, even though she was considered so dangerous that she was not allowed visitors. To pass the time, she read, wrote her diary and taught other prisoners. She also helped to care for a prisoner's baby. Indira expected a long sentence but she was released in May 1943, after eight months.

Two months later, Feroze was also freed and he and Indira went to stay at Anand Bhavan. On 20 August 1944, their first child, a boy called Rajiv, was born. Feroze hoped that now Indira had a baby to look after she would spend more time at home. But even though Indira was devoted to her son, she was too involved in her political work to take a back seat.

On motherhood

'To bring a new being into this world, to see its tiny perfection and to dream of its future greatness is the most moving of all experiences and fills one with wonder and **exaltation**.'

(Indira, on becoming a mother)

Freedom at midnight

By the time World War Two ended in August 1945, it was obvious that Britain could not justify its rule of India for much longer, nor stop the **nationalist** unrest. Steps began to be taken to hand over power. Indira's father, along with the other Congress leaders, was released from prison to take part in talks with the British government. In September 1946, Nehru was asked to head an **interim government**, which would lead India to independence. In effect, he was now prime minister of India.

Official duties

This was an exciting time for Indira. But life was also hectic. Feroze had been appointed to a new job in Lucknow as managing director of the *National Herald,* a Congress newspaper. He and Indira moved to a rented bungalow in Lucknow. But their settled life did not last for long. With his new responsibilities, Nehru's life was now busier than ever. A constant stream of visitors demanded his time, and Indira felt that it was her duty to support and help him. Not for the first time in her life, Indira was torn between her husband and her father. She began to divide her time between Delhi, where Nehru was based, and Lucknow. But it was a night's journey by train between the two cities, and the travelling left Indira exhausted.

TO LOCATE THE PLACES MENTIONED, SEE THE MAP OF INDIA ON PAGE 30.

On 14 December 1946, Indira and Feroze's second son, Sanjay, was born. Indira was thrilled. She doted on her sons. Despite her busy schedule, she tried to make as much time as possible for them. One day, a woman remarked that Indira could not have much time left over from her work to spend with her sons. Sanjay rushed to her rescue with the words: 'My mother does lots of important work, yet she plays with me more than you do with your little boy.'

Independence

On the stroke of midnight on 14–15 August 1947, India became an independent country. Indira was present in the Indian Parliament when her father made his historic speech: 'Long years ago we made a **tryst** with destiny and now the time comes when we shall redeem our pledge, not wholly or in full measure but very substantially. At the stroke of the midnight hour when the world sleeps, India will awake to life and freedom.'

Next day, Nehru was sworn in as the first prime minister of India, and he ceremonially hoisted the **saffron**, white and green Indian flag. History was being made. It was a moment that Indira, then aged 29, never forgot. At last, it seemed that everything she and her family had struggled for was coming to **fruition**.

▼ Lord Mountbatten, the British **viceroy**, announcing Indian independence in 1947.

▲ Jubilant crowds in Bombay, celebrating India's independence in August 1947.

Partition

But there was a price to pay for freedom. India's **Hindus** and **Muslims** were united in their wish for the British to leave. But they disagreed violently about the future of India. The Muslims thought that an India led by Hindus would be as bad for them as one led by the British. For many years, the All-India Muslim League had been campaigning for a separate country for the millions of Indian Muslims. The country was to be called Pakistan, and it would include parts of the states of Punjab in the west and Bengal in the east. It was agreed that India should be partitioned and, on 14 August 1947, Pakistan came into being. It was divided into two parts – West Pakistan and East Pakistan – separated by Indian territory.

TO LOCATE THE PLACES MENTIONED, SEE THE MAP OF INDIA ON PAGE 30.

On independence

'It was impossible to take in that after all these years something we had thought of and dreamt of and worked for ever since I could remember, had happened. It was such a powerful experience that I think I was numb. You know when you go to an extreme of pleasure or pain, there is numbness. Freedom was just so big a thing that it could not register, it seemed to fill all of you and all your world.'

(Indira talking about India's independence)

The partition of India was marked by terrible violence and bloodshed. Many Muslims who found themselves living in the new India fled to Pakistan. And Hindus in the new Pakistan fled to India. Families packed up their belongings, left their homes and desperately tried to escape over the new borders. In the chaos, hundreds of thousands of people were killed as Hindus and Muslims, who had previously lived together in peace, now turned on each other. **Refugees** began pouring into India from Pakistan.

In Delhi, Mahatma Gandhi urged Indira to help in the refugee camps where thousands of people were starving and thirsty and living in filthy conditions. Cholera, typhoid and other

▼ *India and West and East Pakistan after the partition of India in 1947.*

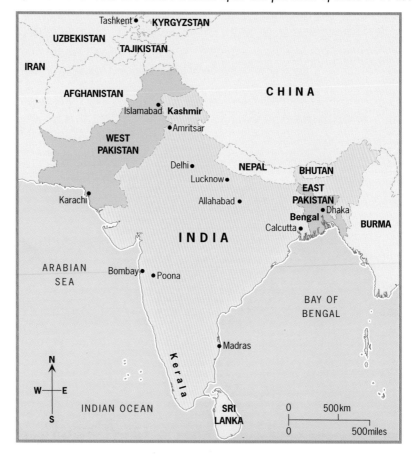

life-threatening diseases spread through the camps like wildfire. Soon Indira was spending up to twelve hours a day in the camps, organizing food, water and medical supplies and trying to reassure the terrified refugees. It was difficult and dangerous work because of the threat of disease and violence. But she was determined to do what she could. Besides, as she once told her father, she coped best in a crisis.

▶ *Muslim refugees from India crowding on to a train bound for Pakistan.*

Key dates: Towards independence

1858	India comes under British Crown rule
1885	The Indian National Congress is founded
1906	The All-India Muslim League is formed
1920	Mahatma Gandhi launches his non-cooperation campaign
1935	The Government of India Act gives Indians a greater say in the government of the country
1942	The 'Quit India' movement is launched to force the British to leave India
1947	India and Pakistan become independent

Entering politics

For the next seventeen years, until her father's death, Indira acted as his official hostess, running his household and accompanying him on foreign trips. She moved to Delhi to be with him, taking Rajiv and Sanjay with her. The prime minister's official residence in Delhi was a magnificent house, called Teen Murti House, or the House of the Three Statues. It was named after the statues of three soldiers that stand on a roundabout at its entrance. In the days of the Raj, it had belonged to the British commander-in-chief.

Keeping house

Keeping house for Nehru was a daunting task. Teen Murti was a huge house, with long corridors and enormous rooms, including a ballroom and a banqueting hall. Indira tried her best to make it feel like home. She replaced the dark oil paintings with Indian pictures and had the walls painted white. Indira was responsible for the whole household. This meant looking after the huge number of guests, working out menus and

▲ Indira (right) with her father, Jawaharlal Nehru, and her eldest son, Rajiv, in 1950, in the grounds of Teen Murti, the prime minister's official residence.

seating plans, supervising the servants and staff, and making sure that her father and sons were cared for. Many of the guests followed special diets and one of her most difficult jobs was making sure that they all got the right thing to eat.

Travelling companion

Indira often travelled abroad with her father. In October 1949, she went with him to the USA on her first official trip abroad. In New York City, she went to art galleries, the theatre and to fashionable restaurants. She also met many important American politicians. Later, she accompanied Nehru to other countries all over the world. It was the best training in politics anyone could have.

In April 1953, Indira, Rajiv and Sanjay sailed to England to attend the coronation of Queen Elizabeth II. Nehru joined them later. After the celebrations, Indira travelled to the USSR for the first time. It was her first trip on her own as the prime minister's daughter. She liked the country very much, and was warmly welcomed in return.

Indian government

India is a **republic** with a parliamentary system of government. There are two Houses of Parliament – the Lok Sabha (House of the People) and the Rajya Sabha (Council of States) – to which the Members of Parliament (MPs) belong. The president is head of state and the prime minister is head of the government. Each of India's 26 states also has its own chief ministers and **legislative assemblies** which are answerable to the central government. All Indians over the age of 18 can vote in the general elections. These are normally held every five years.

India's first general election was held in 1951–52. Many people urged Indira to stand for Parliament, but she refused. She did not feel that she was yet ready for political life. Instead, she worked tirelessly, travelling around the country, campaigning for her father. Congress won the election with a huge majority over the opposition parties, and Nehru was re-elected. But increasingly, Nehru began to turn to Indira for political advice, and she was often asked to stand in for him at political meetings.

In 1955, she was elected as a member of the CWC (Congress Working Party). It was a turning point for Indira. She had finally become a political figure in her own right. Inevitably, there were rumours that Nehru had been planning this all along, and that he had pulled some strings. But, according to Indira, her father's only piece of advice about whether she should enter politics or not had been that she should make up her own mind.

After this, Indira rose quickly through the Congress ranks. On 2 February 1959, she was elected as president of Congress, following in her father's and grandfather's footsteps. She served for just under a year. In her short presidential speech, she asked to be treated like any other ordinary party worker.

◀ *Indira with her sons, Rajiv aged 8 (centre) and Sanjay aged 6 (right), in 1953.*

The death of Feroze

Feroze, meanwhile, had been elected MP for Rae Bareilly near Lucknow. He moved from Lucknow to Delhi, but he did not feel welcome at Teen Murti and lived in his own government bungalow. He only visited Teen Murti to see his sons when they were home from boarding school. Increasingly, Indira

▲ *Indira accompanying her father on a trip to London, England, in 1956.*

and Feroze's marriage was coming under strain. Feroze felt left out of the Nehru family and resented Indira always being at her father's beck and call.

In 1958, Feroze suffered a heart attack. For a short while, he and Indira were reconciled. On a family holiday to Kashmir, they even spoke of building their own house on a plot of land that Feroze had bought. But in September 1960, Feroze suffered another serious heart attack. Indira flew back from Kerala where she had been speaking at a conference. She went straight to Feroze's bedside at the hospital, and sat there all night, holding his hand. He died early the next morning, aged 48.

On the campaign trail

'One of the surprises of this election... has been the very fine work done by Indira. She has worked terribly hard. In Delhi, she used to go out at 8 in the morning and return about 11 at night addressing numerous small meetings and groups. She is reported to be a very effective speaker and is in great demand.'

(Nehru describing how hard Indira campaigned for him during the 1951–2 general election)

▶ *Indira in 1959, having been newly elected as president of the Indian National Congress.*

Indira was shattered. She had not expected to lose her husband so young. For the first few days, as she organized Feroze's funeral, she felt quite numb. Then, when her sons returned to boarding school, she wrote in a letter to Rajiv: 'But now I have begun to cry and don't seem to be able to stop. I have never before known such desolation and grief.'

Losing a father

After Feroze died, Indira threw herself into politics again. She travelled to Mexico, the USA, and Britain. Back in India, trouble was brewing. In October 1962, China invaded northern India. It took the Indian government by surprise, and, as a result, the army was totally unprepared. Indira flew to the front line,

On Feroze's death

'I was actually physically ill. It upset my whole being for years, which is strange, because after all he was very, very ill and I should have expected that he would die. However, it was not just a mental pain, but it was as though somebody had cut me in two.'

(Indira, remembering Feroze's death)

taking **Red Cross** supplies. The Chinese invasion ended as quickly as it had begun, just a few weeks later. But the damage had been done. Nehru was held responsible for the military disaster and his popularity dipped. Some people thought that, at the age of 72, he was too old to be prime minister. His health began to break down and, in January 1964, he suffered a stroke. Nehru was left partially paralysed and confined to a wheelchair. Indira devoted all her energy to looking after him. Then, on the morning of 27 May, Nehru suffered another stroke. He died at 1.44 p.m., without regaining consciousness.

Indira was **inconsolable**. But she was not alone. Her grief was shared by millions of Indians for whom her father had been a hero. More than two million mourners lined the funeral route to pay their last respects. One of the most touching notes of **condolence** came from a child who wrote to Indira: 'I like your father very much…. Do not cry or I will also cry.' Later, Indira scattered her father's ashes in the sacred river at Allahabad, and in Kashmir. Afterwards, she

sank into a deep depression. With her husband and father gone, and her sons growing up (Rajiv was now 20 years old and Sanjay 18), Indira felt more alone than ever.

▶ *The body of Indira's father, Jawaharlal Nehru, lying in state in May 1964. (Indira is on the far left of this picture.)*

Prime Minister Gandhi

With Nehru gone, the battle to succeed him began in earnest. Backed by the most powerful members of Congress, called the 'Syndicate', Lal Bahadur Shastri, a quiet, modest man, was appointed prime minister. Indira moved out of Teen Murti House and into a spacious government bungalow at 1 Safdarjung Road. The new prime minister did not want to live in Teen Murti, and the house was later turned into the Nehru Museum.

▲ Lal Bahadur Shastri, prime minister of India from 1964 to 1966.

Shastri invited Indira to become minister of information and broadcasting in his **Cabinet**. It was her first government post. In order to become a minister, Indira had first to become a Member of Parliament. She was appointed to the Rajya Sabha, the upper house of the Indian Parliament. Indira worked hard at her new job. She relaxed the film censorship laws, extended broadcasting hours, and championed the use of television and radio in education. But Shastri also recognized her usefulness as an ambassador for India. She was elegant and charming, and could speak fluent English and French. He sent her on several trips abroad on the government's behalf.

Prime minister

In January 1966, Shastri flew for Tashkent for peace talks with the Pakistani leader over Kashmir. Afterwards, he complained of feeling tired and went to his room. He died later that night of a massive heart attack. He was 61 years old and had been in power for less than two years. When the shocking news reached India, the government was thrown into turmoil once again.

TO LOCATE THE PLACES MENTIONED, SEE THE MAP OF INDIA ON PAGE 30.

This time the Syndicate backed Indira for prime minister. This was largely because they thought that she would be easy to manipulate because of her lack of experience in government. She would also prove a certain vote winner in the next general election, thanks to the magic of the Gandhi and Nehru names. In the Congress election, Indira defeated her closest rival, Morarji Desai, by 186 votes, and became India's first woman prime minister. But the Syndicate had seriously underestimated her. Indira was nobody's puppet. She might have lacked experience, but beneath her reserved exterior, she had a sharp mind, learned quickly and had enormous courage and determination. What's more, she firmly believed that she was the only person who could lead India.

Indira's political skills were soon put to the test. India had suffered a terrible **drought** and many states were facing **famine**. In some places the rice harvest had failed for two years, leading to unrest and rioting. Foreign aid was desperately needed, and in March 1966, Indira visited the USA for talks with President Lyndon Johnson.

▲ *Prime Minister Indira Gandhi (centre) with President and Mrs Lyndon Johnson during a visit to the USA in 1966.*

President Johnson promised to give India three million tonnes of food and $9 million in aid. In return, he wanted Indira and her government to be less critical of the USA's involvement in the **Vietnam War**. Indira agreed to this, but back in India was criticized by Congress for appearing to go against government policy. Indira argued that she was doing what she had to do for the good of the country. But her troubles were just beginning.

At the same time, Indira established closer relations with the USSR, then the USA's arch-enemy. She thought India would benefit from having such a powerful ally. The two countries issued a joint statement denouncing the USA's bombing of Vietnam. The Americans were furious and backed down on their promise of aid. With the general election only months away, Indira found herself with enemies at home and abroad.

Indira's qualities

'She knows all the world leaders, has travelled widely with her father, has grown up amongst the great men of the freedom movement, has a rational and modern mind, is totally free of any **parochialism** – state, **caste** or religion. She has probably inherited her father's scientific temper [logical, ordered mind] and, above all, she can win the election of 1967.'

(K. Kamaraj, a leading Indian politician, on the decision to back Indira as prime minister)

Second term

In the run-up to the 1967 general election, Indira travelled thousands of kilometres across India campaigning for votes. She spoke at hundreds of meetings and drew huge crowds. For Indira, it was always vital to keep in touch with the ordinary people of India. This time, she wanted to be elected to the post of prime minister not just by her party, but by her country. In her campaign speeches, she spoke in simple language, so that ordinary people could understand. They were her family, she said, and she would look after them. In return, the people gave her a new title – 'Mother Indira'.

▶ A poster encouraging Indians to vote for Indira Gandhi and the **Congress Party** in the 1967 general election.

The Congress Party won the 1967 general election, but with the loss of 95 seats. By contrast, Indira was more popular than ever and won her seat with an increased majority. She was re-elected party leader and prime minister. In a shrewd move, she appointed her arch-rival, Morarji Desai, as deputy prime minister.

The party splits

But there were deep divisions within the Congress Party between Indira's supporters and enemies. Matters came to a head in May 1969, when the president of India (the head of state) died suddenly. Indira's choice of candidate to succeed him was the vice-president, V. V. Giri. But her enemies in Congress did not agree. They wanted to nominate one of their own members, Sanjiva Reddy. Indira decided that the time had come to get tough and to stamp her own mark. First she pushed through plans to **nationalize** India's banks. This was popular with ordinary people but not with Congress. Next, she announced that Giri would stand against Reddy. It was a huge risk but it paid off, and Giri was elected. Many of the Congress leaders were furious and accused Indira of acting against the interests of the party.

In November 1969, the Congress Party split into two factions – Congress (O) and Congress (R). Congress (O), or Old Congress, was the old guard, led by Morarji Desai. Indira led Congress (R), or Ruling Congress. But Indira's position was still uncertain. With Congress (O) determined to get rid of her once and for all, Indira made her surprise move. She called a general election for March 1971, a year earlier than expected. She would ask the Indian people to decide her future.

Indira campaigned tirelessly for the 1971 election, touring the country and addressing millions of people. With her campaign slogan of 'Garibi Hatao', or 'Remove Poverty', she pledged to do more to help India's poor. It proved to be a vote winner. When the results of the election were declared, Indira's Congress (R) had won a landslide victory. Indira was back in power, and more popular than ever.

Bangladesh

Since Pakistan's creation in 1947, there had been conflict between the two parts of the country. East and West Pakistan were more than 1,500 kilometres apart, on opposite sides of India. They did not even share a common language – Urdu was spoken in West Pakistan, Bengali in the east. West Pakistan, under a **military dictatorship**, was larger and richer. It dominated the poorer east, and resentment grew. The East Pakistanis began to demand their freedom.

▼ *Indira being sworn in as prime minister in 1971.*

TO LOCATE THE PLACES MENTIONED, SEE THE MAP OF INDIA ON PAGE 30.

In 1971, civil war broke out between East and West Pakistan. West Pakistani troops were sent into Dhaka, the East Pakistani capital, to restore law and order. India gave its backing to East Pakistan and accepted the millions of **refugees** who began to pour across the border. In December, West Pakistan declared war on India and its airforce bombed nine Indian air bases. But Indira was ready. She immediately sent Indian troops to East Pakistan to put down the West Pakistani forces and support the **freedom fighters**. On 16 December 1971, the West Pakistani army surrendered, and East Pakistan became the independent country of Bangladesh.

Free Bangladesh

'I have an announcement to make, which I think the House has been waiting for, for some time. The West Pakistan forces have unconditionally surrendered in Bangladesh.... Dhaka is now the free capital of a free country. This House and the entire nation rejoice in this historic event. We hail the people of Bangladesh in their hour of triumph.'

(Indira speaking to the Indian Parliament on the surrender of the Pakistani army on 16 December 1971)

It was Indira's finest hour. In both India and Bangladesh, she was hailed as a heroine for winning the war and helping to liberate a nation. She had shown that she could be tough and shrewd, and a strong leader. Indeed, many people were calling her the greatest leader India had ever had.

Work and family

As prime minister, Indira's day began early, at about 6 a.m. First she did yoga exercises for about 20 minutes. Then she ate breakfast on a tray in her bedroom, while reading

▲ *Indira shaking hands with Sheikh Mujibur Rahman, the first prime minister of Bangladesh, in 1972.*

the newspapers. Then she met her private secretary to run through the day's schedule. Afterwards, Indira held her morning darshan (public audience) in the garden of 1 Akbar Road. This was the bungalow next door to her own house where she had her offices. For an hour, people from all walks of life could come to meet the prime minister and tell her about their problems. By 10 a.m., Indira was usually at her desk. She went home to 1 Safdarjung Road for lunch at 1 p.m., then returned to her office to work until 7 or 8 p.m. After dinner with the family, she carried on working until midnight, or entertained visitors. She rarely managed more than 5–6 hours' sleep a night, but could nap anywhere.

By now, Indira was sharing her home at 1 Safdarjung Road with her elder son, Rajiv, and his Italian wife, Sonia. Sonia and Indira got on very well, and Indira doted on her two grandchildren, Rahul and Priyanka, who often slept in her room at night. Sonia quickly adapted to Indian life and ran the Gandhi household. After their marriage in 1974, Sanjay, Indira's younger son, and his wife Maneka, also lived at home.

New challenges

In 1972, Indira faced a new challenge. The country suffered a terrible **drought** when the **monsoon** rains failed. The result was a poor harvest and serious food shortages. At the same time, the economic situation was getting worse. Prices rose sharply, and **corruption** flourished. India was in a state of turmoil, with widespread food riots, strikes, and **industrial unrest**. In 1973 and 1974, the monsoon failed again. What had happened to Indira's election promises? The poor were now worse off than ever. Indira's campaign slogan came back to haunt her. In place of 'Garibi Hatao' ('Remove Poverty'), her opponents were chanting 'Indira Hatao' ('Remove Indira') instead.

▼ *Indira declaring the state of emergency in 1975 in Delhi.*

Then came another blow. In 1975, the High Court found Indira guilty of corruption during the 1971 election campaign. Her opponents demanded that she resign but Indira refused. She felt it was her duty to stay and lead her country. On 26 June 1975, she declared a state of emergency, claiming that India's security was being threatened by forces inside and out. Her conviction was overturned, but the state of emergency remained.

Ruthless streak

The state of emergency showed Indira's ruthless streak. It involved the mass arrest of thousands of opposition leaders and demonstrators. The press was harshly censored, and strikes, **sit-ins** and demonstrations were declared illegal and quickly crushed. Indira often acted on her own, by-passing Parliament. Her opponents described her as a **dictator**, bent on destroying India's **democracy**. At first, many of these measures proved popular, restoring law and order to India's riot-torn cities. But things were soon to go disastrously wrong.

During the state of emergency, Indira began to rely more and more on the advice of her younger son, Sanjay. Her actions had left her isolated from her colleagues, and she needed someone she could trust and confide in. Indira made no secret that she was grooming Sanjay to succeed her. But Sanjay was no Indira or Nehru. Many people thought that he was arrogant and irresponsible, a **playboy** who preferred driving fast cars and flying planes to hard work. Sanjay's increasing hold over his mother worried them. But few dared speak out openly against the prime minister's son. And even if Indira was aware of her son's behaviour, she turned a blind eye.

▲ *Indira with her son, Sanjay, in January 1980. Sanjay's influence was damaging for Indira and for India as a whole.*

It was Sanjay who introduced the two most disastrous policies of the state of emergency – family planning and slum clearance. In theory, everyone agreed with the need for better birth-control and housing policies. India's population was rising fast, by about twelve million people a year. If the poor were to be helped, population growth had to be slowed down. But the way in which Sanjay put his policies into practice appalled even Indira's closest allies. And it was the poor – the very people who Indira had claimed the state of emergency would help – who suffered most.

Terrified villagers were rounded up and forced to have an operation to **sterilize** them. In return, they were given money, a tin of cooking oil, or a radio. City slums were brutally cleared without any thought of where the slum-dwellers would go. In Delhi, a large, rambling area of tumbledown houses and shacks had grown up around the Jama Masjid, the city's old main **mosque**. People had lived here for centuries. But Sanjay did not care. He ruthlessly ordered the buildings to be demolished for the sake of the 'beautification of Delhi'.

Householders and shopkeepers were given only an hour or so to clear out before the bulldozers moved in. When people protested, the police opened fire on them.

The aftermath

Criticized at home and abroad, Indira could no longer ignore what was happening. Sanjay, and the state of emergency, were spiralling out of control and doing untold harm to Indira. Instead of getting rid of poverty, her opponents said, she was getting rid of the poor. Indira's love of Sanjay had blinded her to his faults. She was now more unpopular than ever and had lost the respect of those that mattered – the ordinary people of India. In January 1977, Indira relaxed the state of emergency, released the political leaders, and called a general election for March. But Sanjay and the state of emergency had turned the people against her. Congress suffered a heavy defeat and Indira lost her seat. Her bitter enemy, Morarji Desai, was sworn in as leader of the newly-formed Janata Party, and became prime minister.

▼ *Opposition leader, Morarji Desai, addressing a rally as campaigning began for the 1977 general election.*

For the first time in her life, Indira had become a political outsider. She also found herself homeless. She left 1 Safdarjung Road, which belonged to the government, and moved into the house of an old family friend. But she was determined to fight back. In May 1977, she formed her own new party, called Congress I (Indira). In the state elections of February 1978, the party fielded several candidates, including Indira. She contested and won a seat in Karnataka, southern India, and was re-elected to Parliament as an MP.

◀ *Indira campaigning during the 1978 state elections. She was re-elected to Parliament as MP for Karnataka.*

Return to power

By 1980, the ruling Janata Party, led by Morarji Desai, was in disarray. It had no real policies and failed to keep its promises of helping India's poor. Once again, the country was in chaos, with soaring prices, a rising crime rate and a poor economy. In 1979, Desai resigned as prime minister and was succeeded by Charan Singh. He dissolved Parliament and called a general election for January 1980.

TO LOCATE THE PLACES MENTIONED, SEE THE MAP OF INDIA ON PAGE 30.

Meanwhile, Indira was hard at work saving her reputation. She travelled all over India, and was given a warm welcome wherever she went. With the Janata Party in a shambles, many people felt that Indira was the only person who really

► *Indira waving to the crowds as she tours India to win support for her Congress I party.*

understood India. In the elections, Congress I won with a large majority. At 62 years of age, Indira became prime minister for a fourth term. It was a sensational comeback. Sanjay also won his seat and continued to be his mother's closest advisor. But Indira did not give him a post in her new **Cabinet**. Perhaps she realized what people would say. Instead she appointed him general secretary of the party, a post she herself had held.

But the joy of her victory was short-lived. On 23 June 1980, Sanjay was killed in a plane crash. He was 33 years old. His death stunned Indira. Friends said that she never really recovered from this tragedy. Sanjay had been her favourite son and most trusted advisor. She had depended on him utterly. Who could she turn to now? Desperate to keep the family tradition going, she persuaded a relucant Rajiv to resign his job as an airline pilot and join the **Congress Party**. In 1981, Rajiv was elected to his brother's vacant seat in Parliament.

Key dates: Indira's terms of office

1966–1967	First term
1967–1971	Second term
1971–1977	Third term
1980–1984	Fourth term

▲ Indira listening to a Sikh man's grievances during her daily darshan (audience) a few weeks before her death.

Operation Blue Star

Over the next few years, Indira faced new calls for independence from several Indian states who did not feel that their needs were being met by the central government. In the Punjab, trouble was brewing as a group of **militant Sikhs**, led by Jarnail Singh Bhindranwale, demanded a separate Sikh state. The Sikh religion had been founded in the Punjab in the 16th century, and its millions of followers still lived largely in the state. Bhindranwale and his heavily-armed followers occupied the Golden Temple in Amritsar, the Sikhs' most sacred shrine. From here, they waged a war of violence and **terrorism** against the government. When negotiations broke down, it was clear to Indira that drastic action was needed.

On 6 June 1984, Indira sent the Indian army into the Golden Temple to remove Bhindranwale and his men. Operation Blue Star, the campaign's official government name, had begun. In the fighting that followed, up to 1000 Sikhs, including Bhindranwale, and 300 soldiers were killed. The Golden Temple was badly damaged and the Akal Takht, its most sacred shrine, was riddled with bullet holes. The Sikhs swore to get their revenge for the devastation of their holiest place.

Assassination

After Operation Blue Star, Indira knew that her life was in danger from Sikhs wanting revenge. On the morning of 31 October 1984, she left home to go to her office, a few minutes' walk away, for a television interview. Since Operation

Addressing the nation

'Indira Gandhi has been assassinated. She was mother not only to me but to the whole nation. She served the Indian people to her last drop of blood.... We can and must face this tragic ordeal with **fortitude**, courage and wisdom.'

(Rajiv Gandhi in a speech to the people following his mother's death, 1984)

Blue Star, she had taken to wearing a bullet-proof vest, but she had not put it on today. As she reached the garden gate, she turned to greet her Sikh bodyguards – Beant Singh, who had worked for her for many years, and a younger man, Satwant Singh. Without warning, Beant Singh pulled out his revolver and pointed it at Indira. Then he shot her at point-blank range. Satwant Singh also opened fire. Indira fell to the ground. In the chaos that followed, Beant Singh and Satwant Singh were arrested and a car called to rush Indira to hospital. At 2.23 p.m., Indira Gandhi was pronounced dead.

On the evening of his mother's death, Rajiv was sworn in as Congress president and prime minister of India. One of his first acts was to try to stop the rioting sparked off by Indira's death. In Delhi and other Indian cities, some 2500 people were killed, as angry **Hindus** attacked Sikhs. Because of the unrest, few people lined the Delhi streets as Indira's funeral cortege passed by, carrying her body to the cremation grounds on the banks of the Jumna River in Delhi. It was the end of an extraordinary life.

◀ *Indira's funeral procession in November 1984.*

Impact and legacy

As the first woman prime minister of India, traditionally a **male-dominated society**, Indira Gandhi undoubtedly earned her place in history. But opinion was, and continues to be, divided about her lasting legacy. Loved and loathed in equal measure, Indira was an intriguing mixture – a strong and ruthless political leader, but also a warm and loving mother and doting grandmother.

During her lifetime

As prime minister, Indira had many achievements to her name. She was leader of the world's largest **democracy** and, despite its vast size and the frequent outbreaks of religious unrest, managed to keep it largely united. Her regular trips abroad helped to get India noticed on the international stage, strengthening relationships with foreign powers that her father had begun. But her ruthless handling of the state of emergency earned her many lasting enemies who accused her of acting like a **dictator**. In her personal life, her indulgence of her son, Sanjay, did her untold harm, and she was criticized for trying to build a ruling **dynasty**, rather than a democracy. In later years, her determination to rule India from the centre caused great resentment among the states, and this resentment led ultimately to her death.

◀ *The Indira Gandhi memorial, photographed in 1997.*

Thoughts of death

'If I die a violent death, as some fear and a few are plotting, I know the violence will be in the thought and action of the assassin, not in my dying – for no hate is dark enough to overshadow the extent of my love for my people and my country. No force is strong enough to divert me from my purpose and my endeavour to take this country forward.'

(Indira in 1984)

◀ *Indira speaking in Jaipur in 1984, a short time before her death. Her legacy remains as one of India's most remarkable leaders.*

After her death

Since her death, Indira's influence has continued to be felt across India. Thousands of places are named after her – airports, hospitals, museums, schools and colleges. But today the **Congress Party**, which she led for so long, is a spent force. After Indira, Congress lost the 1989 elections and Rajiv, her successor, was assassinated in 1991 while campaigning. Today his wife, Sonia Gandhi, is president of Congress and leader of the opposition in the Indian Parliament. Will the Nehru-Gandhi dynasty continue? Some people think that Indira's grandchildren might be persuaded to enter politics in the future. Others think that the family's and the party's time has passed.

Despite the highs and lows that marked her personal and political life, there is no doubt that Indira Gandhi was a remarkable leader. She genuinely loved India and believed that she was doing her best for her country. In her last speech, made the day before she died, Indira said: 'I shall continue to serve until my last breath and, when I die, I can say that every drop of my blood will **invigorate** India and strengthen it.'

Timeline

1917	Indira Priyadarshini Nehru is born in Allahabad, India, on 19 November.
1919	The Amritsar massacre.
1920	Mahatma Gandhi launches his campaign of non-violent disobedience ('satyagraha') to protest against British rule in India.
1926	Indira sails to Europe with her parents. She goes to school in Switzerland.
1929	Indira forms the Monkey Army.
1931	Motilal Nehru, Indira's grandfather, dies.
1934	Indira enrols at Santiniketan university.
1935	Indira travels to Europe with her mother.
1936	Kamala, Indira's mother, dies in Switzerland. Indira goes to Badminton School, England.
1937	Indira begins her studies at Somerville College, Oxford.
1939–45	World War Two.
1941	Indira returns to India.
1942	The 'Quit India' Campaign. Indira marries Feroze Gandhi. Indira and Feroze are arrested and sent to jail.
1943	Indira is released from prison.
1944	First son, Rajiv, is born.
1946	Second son, Sanjay, is born.
1947	India becomes independent. Jawaharlal Nehru becomes prime minister. India is partitioned and the new country of Pakistan created.
1948	Mahatma Gandhi is assassinated.
1955	Indira is elected to the Congress Working Committee (CWC).
1959	Indira is elected president of Congress.
1960	Feroze Gandhi dies.
1962	China invades northern India.
1964	Jawaharlal Nehru dies. Lal Bahadur Shastri becomes prime minister. Indira becomes minister of information and broadcasting.
1966	Following Shastri's death, Indira is sworn in as prime minister of India.
1967	Indira wins a second term in office.

1971	Civil war in Pakistan. East Pakistan becomes Bangladesh.
1971	Indira wins a third term in office.
1975	Indira declares a state of emergency.
1977	The state of emergency is ended. Indira is defeated in the general election. Morarji Desai becomes prime minister.
1980	Indira returns to power for a fourth term. Sanjay Gandhi dies in a plane crash.
1984	Indira sends troops into the Golden Temple in Amritsar to put down Sikh militants. Indira is assassinated by her Sikh bodyguards. Rajiv Gandhi becomes prime minister.

Key people of Gandhi's time

Desai, Morarji (1896–1995). Prime minister of India from 1977–9. As leader of the Janata Party, he became prime minister after Indira Gandhi's defeat in the general election. An arch enemy of Indira's, he resigned from office in 1979 after a vote of no-confidence was taken against him.

Gandhi, Feroze (1912–60). Husband of Indira Gandhi and father of Rajiv and Sanjay. He married Indira in 1942. He died of a heart attack in September 1960.

Gandhi, Mohandas K. (1869–1948). Born in Gujarat, western India, Gandhi practised as a barrister in England and South Africa, where he led the non-violent struggle for the civil rights of Indian workers. Later, as leader of the movement for Indian independence, he applied the technique of 'satyagraha', or non-violent protest, to the freedom struggle. A close friend of the Nehru family, he was assassinated in 1948 by a Hindu extremist. He was known as Mahatma, which means 'Great Soul'.

Gandhi, Rajiv (1944–91). Indira Gandhi's eldest son. Prime minister of India from 1984–9. Until 1981 he worked as an airline pilot, then was elected to Parliament and became a close advisor to his mother. He was elected as prime minister and leader of Congress I when Indira was assassinated. He was assassinated in 1991 during an election rally.

Gandhi, Sanjay (1946–80). Indira Gandhi's youngest son who became her closest political ally. In the state of emergency, Sanjay was responsible for two disastrous policies – family planning and slum clearance – which led to his mother's fall from power. He was killed in a plane crash in 1980.

Nehru, Jawaharlal (1889–1964). Indira Gandhi's father and the first prime minister of independent India. He served as prime minister from 1947 to the time of his death in 1964. Educated at Harrow public school and Cambridge University in England, Nehru joined his father's legal practice in India and worked as a barrister. After the Amritsar **massacre**, he joined the independence movement and became a staunch supporter and close friend of Mahatma Gandhi. As a leader of the Indian National Congress, he spent a great deal of Indira's childhood in jail.

Nehru, Motilal (1861–1931). Indira Gandhi's grandfather and father of Jawaharlal Nehru. Motilal came from a wealthy Kashmiri family. He settled in Allahabad where he established a prosperous legal practice. A follower of Western ways, he later gave up his practice and became active in the independence movement.

Pandit, Vijayalakshmi (1900–90). Jawaharlal's sister and Indira's aunt. She played a prominent role in the independence movement and in the women's movement. In her political life, she served as Indian ambassador to the USSR, the USA, Ireland and Spain.

Shastri, Lal Bahadur (1904–66). Became prime minister of India in June 1964 after Jawaharlal Nehru's death. Born in Benares, he entered politics after leaving university and joined the Indian National Congress in the 1920s. He was active in the independence movement and was jailed several times. After independence, he served as minister of police and transport of the state of Uttar Pradesh, and later ran various ministries in the central government. He died in Tashkent, in January 1966, having just signed a peace treaty with Pakistan.

Tagore, Rabindranath (1861–1941). Great Indian poet, novelist, playwright, philosopher and painter. Born in Calcutta, he studied law in England, then returned to India. In 1901 he established the Viswa Bharati University at Santiniketan in West Bengal as a centre of universal learning. In 1913 he was awarded the Nobel Prize for Literature. He wrote the national anthems of India, Bangladesh and Sri Lanka. A firm supporter of Indian **nationalism**, he renounced the knighthood given to him by the British after the Amritsar massacre.

Places to visit and further reading

Places to visit
Sansad Bhavan (Parliament House), Sansad Marg, New Delhi, India
Rashtrapati Bhavan (the residence of the Indian president), Raj Path, New Delhi, India
Nehru Museum, Teen Murti Bhavan, Teen Murti Road, New Delhi, India
Indira Gandhi's home, 1 Safdarjang Road, New Delhi, India

Websites
BBC history website
www.bbc.co.uk/education
Biographical articles on the internet:
www.nielindia.com/biographies/indiragandhi.html
www.cncw.com/india/indira.html
Articles on Indian independence from a website created by the University of California, Los Angeles:
www.sscnet.ucla.edu/southasia/history/independent/indira.html
Articles on India's politics, people and constitution:
www.goidirectory.nic.in
Heinemann Explore, an online resource for Key Stage 3 history:
www.heinemannexplore.co.uk

Further reading
Such a Long Journey, Rohinton Mistry, Faber, 1991
A Fine Balance, Rohinton Mistry, Faber, 1996
An Autobiography or The Story of My Experiments with Truth, M. K. Gandhi, Penguin, 1982
Autobiography, Jawaharlal Nehru, Bodley Head, 1936
The Discovery of India, Jawaharlal Nehru, Signet Press, 1946

Sources
The New India, Ved Mehta, Penguin, 1971
Indira Gandhi, Trevor Drieberg, Vikas Publications, 1972
The Turbulent Years, Rani Dube, Quartet, 1978
The Nehrus and the Gandhis, Tariq Ali, Picador, 1985
The Cambridge Encyclopedia of India, Cambridge University Press, 1989
Indira, Katherine Frank, HarperCollins, 2001

Glossary

ancestor relative who died a long time ago

ballot votes cast in an election

boycott refuse to buy or use something

Cabinet group of senior politicians who lead the government

caste one of the four classes or groups into which Hindu society is traditionally divided

civil war war between different groups of people living in the same country

condolence expressing sympathy for someone who is unhappy because a loved one has died

Congress Party leading political party of India for most of the time since independence. It began as the Indian National Congress in 1885.

corruption dishonesty, such as taking bribes

democracy form of government in which the people of a country vote for their leaders

dictator ruler who does not allow ordinary people to have any say in how their country is governed

disperse scatter or spread out

dock place in a law court where the accused person stands

drought long period of time during which no rain falls

dynasty series of rulers belonging to the same family

empire group of countries ruled by a single state. After World War One, the British Empire governed over a quarter of the world's population.

exaltation feeling of great happiness or joy

famine when food is very short and people are starving

fortitude great strength and courage

freedom fighters people who fight and struggle to help their country gain independence

fruition when something that has been planned actually happens

Gandhi cap white, peaked cap worn by Mahatma Gandhi and his followers

Hindi one of the most important and widely spoken Indian languages

Hindu follower of Hinduism, or the Hindu religion, which began and is still largely practised in India

inconsolable too upset to be consoled, or comforted

industrial unrest when workers go on strike, shops and factories close, and transport systems do not run

interim government government which fills in for a short time until a permanent government is elected

invigorate make someone feel more lively or energetic

khadi type of rough, homespun cloth

legislative assemblies groups within a country's government that make and pass laws

male-dominated society society in which most of the important jobs are held by men

massacre brutal or violent killing of a large number of people

militant person who is outspoken or even violent in the way in which he or she supports a cause

military dictatorship government of a country by the leader of the army or armed forces

monsoon heavy rains which farmers in certain parts of the world rely on for watering their crops

mosque building in which Muslims meet to pray

Muslim follower of the religion of Islam, the second largest religion in India, next to Hinduism

nationalist person who believes that the peoples of the world are made up of distinct nations, each of which ought to have its own state

nationalize change the ownership and control of industries or businesses from private hands to control by the government

parochialism narrow-minded view

Parsi follower of the Zoroastrian religion which began in Persia about 3,000 years ago. A large Parsi community lives in western India.

playboy man, often with plenty of money, who enjoys going out to clubs, bars and so on

Red Cross organization set up to help the victims of war or other disasters all over the world

refugees people who have fled from their own country to another country because of war or another disaster

republic form of government in which the people or their elected politicians have power

saffron yellowish-orange colour. A sacred colour for Indian religions.

sanatorium clinic which specializes in treating people with illnesses such as tuberculosis

sari traditional dress worn by Indian women, made from a long piece of cloth wound around the body

Sikh follower of the Sikh religion which began in Punjab, India in the 16th century

sit-in form of protest in which people sit in a public place and refuse to move

sterilize give people an operation which means that they cannot have children

terrorism campaign of violence and intimidation

tryst secret appointment to meet someone

tuberculosis disease which affects the lungs

verandah open balcony or gallery built along the side of a house

viceroy official who governs a country in the name of another country's king, queen or government

Vietnam War war fought between 1954 and 1975 between North and South Vietnam. From 1961, the USA sent troops to Vietnam to support the South Vietnamese.

Index